At the Wind's Will by Louise Chandler Moulton

I had walked on at the wind's will, —
I sat now, for the wind was still.
D. G. Rossetti

Ellen Louise Chandler Moulton was born on 10th April 1835 in Pomfret, Connecticut.

At her peak she was one of America's most popular children's authors but her works also included many stories and novels for adults, volumes on travels, the editing and prefacing of biographies and, of course, her poetry.

She published her first work, some verses, in a local newspaper when she was 15. Three years later, a Boston company published her 'This, That, and the Other,' a collection of stories and poems which had previously in magazines and periodicals. After publication Moulton went for a year to Emma Willard's Troy Female Seminary and left in 1855. Six weeks after leaving, on August 27th, 1855, she married the Boston publisher, William Upham Moulton. He was instrumental in developing her literary career although the Civil War would interrupt her work until the early 1870s.

Her poems and stories were also much requested by the leading magazines of the day including Harper's Magazine, The Atlantic, The Galaxy and Scribner's.

As the Boston correspondent for the New York Tribune she wrote regular detailed critiques from 1870 to 1876.

In the winter of 1876, her first volume of 'Poems' (renamed 'Swallow Flights' in England), was published and highly praised by the critics.

It was not until she was 41 that she first travelled to London and on to Europe. Thereafter she more often than not spent summers abroad and winters in Boston. She made friends easily with the literary giants of her day and in turn her work was admired by them.

For the Boston Herald Sunday issue she wrote a weekly literary letter from 1886 to 1892.

Ellen Louise Chandler died after a lengthy illness on 10th August 1908 in Boston, Massachusetts. She was 78.

TO HOPE

Undying Hope, Memory's immortal heir,
To thee I consecrate this sheaf of song, —
In darkest gloom of thee I am aware;
Thy magic is to make the weak soul strong.

Index of Contents

AT THE WIND'S WILL

So far, so far have I come,
Blown by the Wind of Fate:
Whither t The Voice is dumb. —
The Silence dismays me, I wait.

The Sunshine mocks me at morn.
The Stars deride me at night;
Shall strength in my soul be born
To triumph over their slight t

Shall I live when their fires are out?
Shall I reach where they cannot go?
Ah, Fate, resolve me the doubt, —
Blow on, strong Wind! I will know.

LYRICS

In the world of dreams I have chosen my part
To sleep for a season, and hear no word
Of true love's truth, or of light love's art,
Only the song of a secret bird.
A. C. Swinburne.

Shall I not tell my dream in a song?
Philip Bourke Marston.

AT THE WIND'S WILL

SONGS AT SEA

I have been lonely the whole day long;
Come and find me to-night with a song;
Sing to me now, when the wind is low,
And my heart shall answer as on we go;
Listen and answer, and none shall know.

Over the brooding, wonderful sea
The song that is sung alone for me
Floats, and none other its strain can hear,
Or catch the music, subtle and dear,
Of the delicate singing that seeks my ear.

The West is red with the sunset's glow;
In the East the moon is hanging low;
And fast and far the light winds flee,
As I sail, with your songs for company,
'Twixt the silent sky and the silent sea.

Do these birds of song need a sheltering nest?
See! I will hide them warm in my breast;
There shall they fold their venturous wing,
And all the night through nestle and sing
Songs of love and of sorrowing.

Then, when the morning is young and gay,
Up from their shelter and far away!
And, like carrier doves, they shall bear as they flee
The echoes of all they have sung to me
Alone with the night and the wind and the sea; —

The echoes of passion's divine despair,
The bliss and the bane of a lover's prayer,
All the delicate singing that none might hear;
And the answer my heart shall send, my dear,
On the breath of the morning fine and clear.

ON A ROSE PRESSED IN A BOOK

I win the summer back again
At touch of this dead rose. —
O lavish joy! O tender pain!
The very June wind blows,
And thrills me with the old refrain
Whose music my heart knows:
I win the summer back again
At touch of this dead rose.

Ah, lost is all the summer's gain,
And lost my heart's repose;
And was it tears or was it rain
That wept the season's close?
The winter suns they coldly wane;
White fall the winter snows:
But Love and Summer come again
At touch of this dead rose.

THE SUN IS LOW

I sit and wait for you, Dear, my Dear,
Now the sun is low;
From the far-off town the path runs clear,
And the way you know —

The old, old way that brought you here,
In the Long-Ago.

The white moon climbs, and looks at me -
Her smile is cold;
Something she sees that I do not see —
The moon is old.

I catch a sigh from the winds that flee
Across the wold —
What is the secret they hide from me? —
They have not told.

To Lethe-country your steps were set —
Did you taste that spring
That makes the heart of a man forget
The dearest thing?

Nay! I sit and wait for you, Dear, my Dear,
For the sun is low —
From your far-off place the path runs clear,
And you still must know
The old, old way that brought you here
In the Long-Ago.

THE SECRET OF ARCADY

I hied me off to Arcady —
The month it was the month of May,
And all along the pleasant way
The morning birds were mad with glee,
And all the flowers sprang up to see,
As I went on to Arcady.

But slow I fared to Arcady —
The way was long, the winding way —
Sometimes I watched the children play,
And then I laid me down to see
The great white clouds sail over me —
I thought they sailed to Arcady.

Then by me sped to Arcady
Two lovers, each on palfrey gray,
And blithe with love, and blithe with May,
And they were rich, and held in fee
The whole round world: and Youth is he

Who knows the path to Arcady.

I followed on to Arcady —
But I was all alone that day,
And shadows stole along the way,
And somehow I had lost the key
That makes an errant mortal free
Of the dear fields of Arcady.

But still I fared toward Arcady,
Until I slept at set of day,
And in my dreams I found the way;
And all the Fates were kind to me;
So that I woke beneath a tree
In the dear land of Arcady.

What did I find in Arcady? —
Ah, that I never must betray:
I learned the secrets of the May;
And why the winds are fresh and free,
And all the birds are mad with glee
That soar and sing in Arcady.

I dwell no more in Arcady: —
But when the sky is blue with May,
And flowers spring up along the way,
And birds are blithe, and winds are free,
I know what message is for me, —
For I have been in Arcady.

AT NIGHT'S HIGH NOON

Under the heavy sod she lies —
I saw them close her beautiful eyes —
She lies so still, and she lies so deep,
That all of them think she is fast asleep.

I, only, know at the night's high noon
She comes from the grave they made too soon:
I see the light of her cold, bright eyes,
As I see the stars in the wintry skies.

The scornful gleam of an old surprise
Is still alive in those wonderful eyes —
And the mocking lips are ripe and red,
Smiling, still, at the words I said.

She mocks me now, as she mocked me then: —
'Dead is dead,' say the world of men —
But I know when the stars of midnight rise
She shines on me with her cold, bright eyes.

THE VOICE OF SPRING

It was the Voice of Spring —
That faint, far cry —
And birds began to sing,
And winds blew by.

And up the blossoms got —
They knew the call: —
The blue Forget-me-not,
The Lily, tall,

And Mayflowers, pink and white
As any lass,
Sprang up, for heart's delight,
Among the grass.

The happy world is fain
To hail the feet
Of Spring, who comes again,
Spring that is sweet

Let us, dear Heart, rejoice —
You, Love, and I;
We, too, have heard the Voice,
Our Spring is nigh.

IN EXTREMIS

How can I go into the dark,
Away from your clasping hand,
Set sail on a shadowy bark
For the shore of an unknown land?

Your eyes look love into mine;
Your lips are warm on my mouth;
I drink your breath like a wine
Aglow with the sun of the South.

You have made this world so dear!
How can I go forth alone
In the bark that phantoms steer
To a port afar and unknown?

The desperate mob of the dead,
Will they hustle me to and fro,
Or leave me alone to tread
The path of my infinite woe?

Shall I cry, in terror and pain,
For a death that I cannot die,
And pray with a longing vain
To the gods that mock my cry?

Oh, hold me closer, my dear!
Strong is your clasp, — ay, strong,
But stronger the touch that I fear,
And the darkness to come is long.

WHEN LOVE IS YOUNG

In Summer, when the days are long,
The roses and the lilies talk —
Beneath the trees young lovers walk,
And glad birds coo their wooing song.

In Autumn, when the days are brief,
Roses and lilies turn to dust —
Lovers grow old, as all men must,
And birds shun trees that have no leaf.

Then, youth, be glad, in love's brief day!
Pluck life's best blossom while you can
Time has his will of every man —
From leafless hearts love turns away.

AT THE END

Time was when Love's dear ways I used to know —
That time 's at end, and Love has passed me by:
Be merciful, dear God, and let me die —
How can I lift my head from this last blow?

I cannot bear this life whence Faith has fled —
This jostling world in which I walk alone —
Where through long, lonesome nights old memories moan,
With human voices, that the dead is dead.

I cannot bear to meet the day's cold eyes —
The lonesome nights are bitter with my tears —
Shuddering I face the empty hideous years,
Sure that no trumpet 's call will bid my dead arise.

Since Love 's at end, be merciful, oh God! . . . .
I ask no new-born hope, but only this, —
That I may die as died that vanished bliss,
And hide my fruitless pain 'neath some green sod.

Yet there — if the strong soul in me live on —
How deep soe'er the grave, what hope of rest?
Still shall I be discrowned and dispossest,
And find new tortures with new life begun.

The Heavens are deaf! No answer comes to prayer —
I face the cold scorn of the risen day —
Since Love that was my life has turned away,
And left me for companion my Despair.

TO SLEEP

Come Sleep, and kiss mine eyelids down;
Let me forget
Hope's treachery, and Fortune's frown,
And Life 's vain fret.

And would you hold me fast, dear Sleep,
I need not wake,
Since they wake not who used to weep
For my poor sake.

WHEN YOU ARE DEAD

A LOVER SPEAKS

When you are dead, my dainty dear,
And buried 'neath the grass,

Will something of you linger near,
And know me if I pass?

Last night you wore a wild, sweet rose,
To match your sweet, wild grace —
The only flower on earth that grows
I liken to your face.

I would that I that rose had been,
To bloom upon your breast!
One golden hour I should have seen —
What matter for the rest?

To-day you will not grant my prayer,
Or listen while I plead —
But when you dwell alone, down there,
It may be you will heed;

And then your silent heart will stir
With some divine, sweet thrill,
To know that I, your worshipper,
Through death am faithful still;

And something of you, lingering near,
May bless me if I pass —
When you are dead, my dainty dear,
And buried 'neath the grass.

THE BIRDS AND I

A thousand voices whisper it is spring;
Shy flowers start up to greet me on the way,
And homing birds preen their swift wings and sing
The praises of the friendly, lengthening day.

The buds whose breath the glad wind hither bears,
Whose tender secret the young May shall find,
Seem all for me — for me the softer airs,
The gentle warmth, wherewith the day is kind.

Let me rejoice, now skies are blue and bright,
And the round world pays tribute to the spring;
The birds and I will carol our delight,
And every breeze Love's messages shall bring.

What matter though sometimes the cup of tears

We drink, instead of the rich wine of mirth?
There are as many springs as there are years;
And, glad or sad, we love this dear old Earth.

Shall we come back, like birds, from some far sphere —
We and the Spring together — and be glad
With the old joy to hail the sweet young year,
And to remember what good days we had?

THE BIRDS COME BACK

The birds come back to their last year's nest,
And the wild-rose nods in the lane;
And gold in the east, and red in the west,
The sun bestirs him again.

The thief-bee rifles the hawthorn flower;
And the breezes softly sigh
For the columbine in my lady's bower,
And then at her feet they die.

And all the pomp of the June is here —
The mirth and passion and song;
And young is the summer, and life is dear,
And the day is never too long.

Ah! birds come back to their last year's nest,
And the wild-rose laughs in the lane;
But I turn to the east and I turn to the west —
"She never will come again."

A WINTER'S DAWN

After the long and dreary night
I wake to the blessed morning light,
And the white surprise of the snow.
Dreams have mocked me the dark hours through;
And something cried on the winds that blew
Across the country that dreamers know.

Back from the memory-haunted ways
We trod together in by-gone days,
Came a voice — was it yours, my dear? —
Oh, was it yours? Did I hear you plead,

As I heard you once, when I would not heed —
In that far-off land — in that by-gone year?

Wild is my heart, with its hopeless pain —
Oh, for one hour of the past again! —
One brief, bright hour — one least little touch!
Do you forgive me the words I said,
As you look back from the realm of the dead? —

Much is forgiven, when one loves much.
Grief makes wise; for I knew not then,
While you were alive in the world of men,
How the heart of my heart would starve and die,
When you should be gone, beyond my reach,
Where the death-tide breaks on a ghostly beach,
And spirits bereft on the night wind cry.

Spent and done is the lonesome night,
And the sun of the morning is strong and bright —
The sun is bright and the sky is clear —
Yet better the dark, and the winds that blow
Across the country that dreamers know,
And the voice that calls from a by-gone year.

THE LURE

Whence did the music come, my Dear,
That wooed you into the waiting Night,
The song you heard that I could not hear,
The song you followed, my Heart's Delight?

The moon was full, and the sky was clear —
How did you hide from my longing sight?
Into the Dark we vainly peer,
But I looked as vainly into the Light.

Does an echo come to my listening ear
Of music dropped from some far-off height? . . .
Nay, I do but dream, for I did not hear
The song that lured you into the Night.

DEAD MEN'S HOLIDAY

AFTER SHIPKA

Every one kept holiday — except the dead.
Verestschagin

Who dares to say the dead men were not glad,
When all the banners flaunted triumph there
And soldiers tossed their caps into the air,
And cheered, and cheered as they with joy were mad?

Proudly the General galloped down the line,
And shouted thanks and praise to all his men,
And the free echoes tossed it back again,
And the keen air stung all their lips like wine.

And there, in front, the dead lay silently —
They who had given their lives the fight to win —
Were their ears deaf, think you, to all the din,
And their eyes blinded that they could not see?

I tell you, no! They heard, and hearing knew
How brief a thing this triumph of a day,
From which men journey on, the same old way,
The same old snares and pitfalls struggle through.

Theirs the true triumph, for their fight was done;
And with low laughter called they, each to each —
"We are at rest, where foemen cannot reach,
And better this than righting in the sun."

WHEN YOU WERE HERE

When you, my love, were here
My voice was full and loud -
I sang to catch your ear:
Now you are in your shroud
I cannot sing for fear.

That vague world is so near —
Beyond its veil of cloud —
Where you abide, my dear,
If I should sing too loud
Who knows but you would hear?

And then your heart would break
With pity, for 'my sake.

BECAUSE IT IS THE SPRING

I will be glad because it is the spring.
Amy Levy.

Shall I be glad because the year is young?
The shy, swift-coming green is on the trees;
The jonquil's passion to the wind is flung;
I catch the Mayflower's breath upon the breeze.

The birds, aware that mating-time has come,
Swell their plumed, tuneful throats with love and glee;
The streams, beneath the winter's thraldom dumb,
Set free at last, run singing to the sea.

Shall I be glad because the year is young?
Nay; you yourself were young that other year:
Though sad and low the tender songs you sung,
My fond heart heard them, and stood still to hear.

Can I forget the day you said good-by,
And robbed the world and me for alien spheres?
Do I not know, when wild winds sob and die,
Your voice is on them, sadder than my tears?

You come to tell me heaven itself is cold, —
The world was warm from which you fled away, —
And moon and stars and sun are very old —
And you? — oh, you were young in last year's May:

Now you, who were the very heart of spring,
Are old, and share the secrets of the skies;
But I lack something that no year will bring,
Since May no longer greets me with your eyes.

HER PICTURE

Fair face the Greeks had worshipped, have you come
With me to make your home?
You look at me with those deep, haunting eyes,
And all my life replies.

The silence thrills with vague, bewitching tone;
I am no more alone:

I who have sat upon the shore of Time,
Coaxing my lute to rhyme,

Feel in my heart, at impulse of your will,
Youth's eager music thrill;
And since the years have left me not so old,
Now their long tale is told,

But I can love the lovely, and be glad,
I hide the cypress wreath I had
For garland, and adorn me with the rose
That in your garden glows.

A VIOLET SPEAKS

O passer-by, draw near!
Upon a grave I grow;
That she who died was dear
They planted me to show.

Pluck me as you go by —
I am her messenger;
With her sweet breath I sigh;
In me her pulses stir.

Through these my quivering leaves
She fain would speak to you —
She whom the grave bereaves
Of the dear life she knew.

"How glad I was up there!"
She whispers underground.
"Have they who found me fair
Some other fair one found?

"Has he who loved me best
Learned Love's deep lore again,
Since I was laid to rest
Far from the world of men?

"Nay! Surely he will come
To dwell here at the last;
In Death's strange silent home
My hand shall hold him fast

"Yet would that he might know

How hard it is to bide
In darkness here below
And miss him from my side!

"Fain would I send my soul
To lie upon his breast,
And breathe to him Love's whole
That life left unconfest."

Ah, pluck me, passer-by!
For I would bear her breath —
Undying Love's own sigh —
To him who flees from Death.

LEGEND OF A TOMB IN FLORENCE

Here he is, in marble, waiting by a tomb —
Strong-winged for flying, yet, the legends say,
Waiting till a maiden buried here below
Shall break forth and join him once again, some day.

Long ago she lived here, in this Town of Flowers —
She herself a blossom brighter than the rest —
Myrtles blue as Heaven, lilies saintly white,
Ne'er a one was worthy to bloom upon her breast.

Here he saw and loved her — he, the gallant Knight,
Loved this gracious Lady, fairer than the May;
Loved her, and won her, Flower of all Delight —
Then Death, the Robber, stole his love away.

By her grave he waited, years on weary years,
Sure that Love would sometime triumph over Fate,
Till at length, o'er-tired, he too must go to sleep;
Then he bade them carve him, still by her to wait —

But with wings for flying, so that when she came
From her narrow chamber he could bear her high,
Over seas and mountains, past the bars of Earth,
To a spacious dwelling somewhere in the sky.

Still the summons comes not — long their silent dream —
But the watching seraphs pity them, I know,
And the tomb will open, and the dead will rise,
And the Knight and Lady Heavenward will go.

THE SUMMER'S QUEEN

I chant the praises of the regal June,
Fair Queen of all the Twelve months' circling sphere,
Hands full of roses, and sweet lips in tune
To all the mirth and music of the year.

How gay and glad you are, fair Lady mine!
How proud of conquered world and lavish sun,
And air that sparkles like celestial wine,
And laughing streams that frolic as they run!

You sow the fields with lilies — wake the choir
Of summer birds to chorus of delight;
Yours is the year's deep rapture — yours the fire
That burns the West, and ushers in the night —

The short, sweet night — that almost can deceive,
So bright its moon, the birds to sing again,
And fit their morning carols to the eve,
And wake the midnight with the noontide strain.

O June, fair Queen of sunshine and of flowers,
The affluent year will hold you not again —
Once, only once, can Youth and Love be ours,
And after them the autumn and the rain.

BEND LOW AND HARK

Bend low and hark with me, my Dear,
How the winds sigh!
A voice is on them that I fear,
It brings the by-gone days so near,
Like a soul's cry.

Those whom we bury out of sight —
How still they lie!
Beyond the reaches of the Light,
Outside the realm of Day and Night —
Do they not die?

Shall we unbar the long- shut door —
You, Dear, or I? —
Could Love be what Love was before

If we should call them back once more,
And they reply?

Would they Life's largess claim again?
. . . They draw too nigh.
Oh, winds, be still! You shall not pain
My heart with that long-hushed refrain
As you sweep by.

The Dead have had their shining day —
Why should they try
To listen to the words we say —
To breathe their blight upon our May
. . . Yet the winds sigh.

A SONG FOR ROSALYS

Roses lean from their slender stalks —
Oh, but the summer is just begun!
Through her garden Rosalys walks,
And the world is warm with the sun.

Roses and maiden and year
All blooming together;
Heigho, it is good to be here,
In the summer weather!

Love thrives well when the days are long,
And hearts, like the summer, are young and gay.
Words turn to music, and hope grows strong;
But the best is what we can never say.

Oh, once, just once, to be glad once more,
To listen to words that we heard of old,
To steal again through Youth's open door,
And thrill to the story that then was told!

But never twice is a woman young,
And never twice to the year comes June,
And Age is the echo of songs once sung,
With never again the time or the tune.

Roses and maiden and year
All blooming together;
Heigho, it is good to be here,
In the summer weather!

THE GENTLE GHOST OF JOY

A little while ago you knew not I was I —
A little while ago I knew not you were you-
Now the swift hours have run by,
And all the world is new.
I hear the young birds sing
In the rosy light of morn;
Like them I could take wing,
And sing as newly born.

A little while from now I shall be far away —
A little while from now your face I shall not see-
But within my heart a ray
To light the dark will be.
Do you not know that pain
So sad, so sweet, so coy,
That comes, and comes again,
The gentle ghost of Joy?

Ah, that shall dwell with me,
When your face I do not see!

WHEN I WANDER AWAY WITH DEATH

This Life is a fleeting breath,
And whither and how shall I go,
When I wander away with Death
By a path that I do not know?

Shall I find the throne of the Moon,
And kneel with her lovers there
To pray for a cold, sweet boon
From her beauty cold and fair?

Or shall I make haste to the Sun,
And warm at his passionate fire
My heart by sorrow undone,
And sick with a vain desire?

Shall I steal into Twilight-Land,
When the Sun and the Moon are low,
And hark to the furtive band

Of the winds that whispering go —

Telling and telling again,
And crooning with scornful mirth,
The secrets of women and men
They overheard on the earth?

Will the dead birds sing once more,
And the nightingale's note be sad
With the passion and longing of yore,
And the thrushes with joy go mad?

Nay, what though they carol again,
And the flowers spring to life at my feet,
Can they heal the sting of my pain,
Or quicken a dead heart's beat?

What care I for Moon or for stars,
Or the Sun on his royal way?
Only somewhere, beyond Earth's bars,
Let me find Love's long-lost day.

HAS LAVISH SUMMER BROUGHT THE ROSE?

Has lavish summer brought the rose?
A Why did my heart not know,
When every gossip wind that blows
Made haste to tell me so;

And all the birds went mad with glee,
And sang from morn till night;
And then the stars came out to see
What made the world so bright?

But I missed something from the time,
And so I did not guess
The meaning of the summer's rhyme,
Or the warm wind's caress.

Can gladness be where she is not?
Can roses bud and blow?
Does all the world but me forget
What now we must forego?

I care not for the day's kind grace, —
The magic of the night, —

Since with them comes no more the face
That was my heart's delight.

A LOST EDEN

Ah, it was a lonely place,
Where I walked to-day —
That old Garden of Delights,
Where we used to stray.

She is far, whose hand I held
In that bygone time —
Where the summer roses laughed
Clings the winter's rime.

Helen, stately, Helen fair,
Where are you to-night?
Do you gather brighter blooms.
Tranced in new delight?

I remember how you stood —
You who wrought my woe —
Wiling me with strange, sweet smile,
When the sun was low;

And I lingered by your side
Till the stars arose
And looked down with curious eyes
On that Garden Close.

Now you wander, who knows where,
Helen, fair and glad,
Deaf to whispers from the past —
Why should I be sad?

THE MOOD OF A MAN

Through the silence come to mock me
Ancient questions and replies;
A remembered glory blinds me,
From the shining of her eyes.

Though this Southern sun is glowing,
And this alien sky is fair,

Still between me and the sunshine
Waves the pale gold of her hair.

In these unfamiliar places
Her familiar face I see, —
Scornful in its mocking beauty,
Always pitiless for me.

But her scorn no longer moves me —
Reft of hope is free from fear —
So her very coldness warms me,
Her remoteness brings me near.

JUNE'S DAUGHTER

Fair Lady June, proud Queen of all the year,
With blossom-sceptre in thy royal hand —
Vaunt not thyself: though long thy days and dear.
Thy days and thee Time's sway cannot withstand.

Thy splendid sun may kindle the proud morn;
And the high noon may glow with love of thee:
Sunset shall laugh thy longest day to scorn,
And mocking stars its overthrow shall see.

Roses shall wither, though their lavish praise
The nightingales have chanted all night long:
Their fragrant ghosts shall throng the silent ways
Those swift-winged laureates once thrilled with song.

And thou, fair Maid, bright daughter of the June,
Dost thou not know thy youth, like hers, is brief? —
For thee the glad day, and the bird's glad tune;
And then the waning year, the wind-blown leaf.

The rising stars shall mock thy setting sun,
And watch with curious eyes thy fallen state:
Glad month! glad maid! — for both the swift sands run —
And not for month or maid shall Autumn wait.

A SUMMER WOOING

The wind went wooing the rose,
For the rose was fair.

How the rough wind won her, who knows?
But he left her there.
Far away from her grave he blows:
Does the free wind care?

I HAVE CALLED THEE MANY A NIGHT

I have called thee many a night,
While the rest were sleeping;
Thou wert deaf to all I said,
Heedless of my weeping.

Wilt thou never hear again,
Howsoe'er I pray thee?
Then must I go forth to seek,
On thy way waylay thee.

Shall I find, beyond the sun,
Some Celestial Garden?
Shall I kneel there at thy feet,
Clamor for thy pardon?

Nay; how can I wait so long?
Wilt thou not draw near me?
Winged winds are steeds of thine —
Let them hither bear thee.

Long my ear waits for thy words.
How can I forego thee?
Ah! for one brief hour come back,
Let me see and know thee.

THE COQUETTE'S DEFENCE

Red, red roses glowing in the garden,
Rare white lilies swaying on your stalks,
Did you hear me pray my sweet love for pardon,
Straying with him adown your garden walks?

Ah, you glow and smile when the sun shines upon you —
You thrill with delight at the tears of the dew,
And the wind that caresses you boasts that he won you —
Do you think, fair flowers, to them all to be true?

Sun, dew, and wind, ah, they all are your lovers —
Sun, dew, and wind, and you love them back again —
And you flirt with the idle white moth that hovers
Above your sweet beauty, and laugh at his pain.

Must I, then, be deaf to the voices that woo me,
And because I can hear should my sweet Love complain?
Does he not, in forgiving me, stand high above me,
And punish my fault with his gentle disdain?

You trifle, fair flowers, with the many, but one lord
Woos you, and wins you, and conquers the throng —
Dews and winds cool you, for warmth you turn sunward;
You know and I know to whom we belong.

A WHISPER TO THE MOON

Bend low, O Moon, for I fain would tell
My secret to thee, who can keep it well,
And not to the stars that laugh from the sky,
And mock at my pain as they pass me by.

Bend low, pale Moon! Her face is like thine —
Like thine from afar I can see it shine,
Now hid in a cloud, in a halo now —
She is thy kindred; and fickle art thou.

IN VENICE ONCE

In Venice once they lived and loved —
Fair women with their red-gold hair -
Their twinkling feet to music moved,
In Venice where they lived and loved,
And all Philosophy disproved,
While hope was young and life was fair,
In Venice where they lived and loved.

MY QUEEN OF MAY

The laughing garlanded May-time is here;
The glad laburnum whispers at the gate:
"She comes! She comes! I hear her step draw near,

My Queen of Beauty, Arbitress of Fate!"

The lilacs look at her — "She is more fair
Than the white moon, more proud than the strong sun;
Let him who seeks her royal grace beware,
To be unworthy were to be undone."

One wild sweet rose, that dreams the May is June,
Blooms for her; and for her a mateless bird
Thrills the soft dusk with his entrancing tune,
Content if by her only he is heard.

A curious star climbs the far heaven to see
What She it is for whom the waiting night,
To music set, trembles in melody;
Then, by her beauty dazzled, flees from sight.

And I — what am I that ray voice should reach
The gracious ear to which it would aspire?
She will not heed my faltering poor speech;
I have no spell to win what all desire.

Yet will I serve my stately Queen of May;
Yet will I hope, till Hope itself be spent.
Better to strive, though steep and long the way,
Than on some weaker heart to sink content.

WHERE THE NIGHT'S PALE ROSES BLOW

Ah, the place is wild and sweet
Where my darling went: —
If I chase her flying feet
When the day is spent,
Shall I find her, as I go
Where the Night's pale roses blow?

AND YET

Let me forget! Why should I seek to hold
Thine image in the mirror of my mind?
For him who can no way to please thee find
To house such tenant were indeed too bold —
Let me forget!

Do I not know the magic of that smile;
The way that wayward color comes and goes,
Fair Lady of the Lily and the Rose,
What time the souls of men thou would'st beguile:
Do I not know?

Thou shalt not reign, proud Queen, in this poor heart;
No rash oath of allegiance will I swear —
Though thou art beautiful beyond compare,
Thine art is nature, and thy nature art —
Thou shalt not reign!

And yet, and yet — how can I close my door?
It may be thou art weary and acold: —
Come in! Come in! To welcome thee is bold;
But work thy will — I am thy slave once more —
And yet! And yet!

I HEARD A CRY IN THE NIGHT

I heard a cry in the night,
And swift I stole from my bed,
To find her, my heart's delight,
Once more in the lonesome night,
As before they called her dead.

I pulled the curtains away,
I bent my lips to her cheek:
She had fled from the glare of day,
Afar on her lonesome way;
Night came, and I heard her speak.

Again I harked to the call
Of the one little voice so dear;
No matter what might befall,
I had found her, my darling, my all,
And I held her warm and near.

I laid me down by her side:
I cooed like a mother dove.
Ah, was it her lips that replied,
Or only the wind that sighed,
And not my dainty, my love?

For cruel the morning came,
And mocking the blue sky smiled,

And the sun arose like a flame,
And vainly I called her name,
And I wept in vain for my child.

THE NAME ON A DOOR

It is only the name on a door —
Why should there be tears in my eyes?
But I never shall knock there more;
And sorrow is not overwise.

I used to go up the stair
When the day was wearing late,
And come on her unaware
As she sat and dreamed by the grate.

And then, like a sudden flame.
My welcome flashed from her eyes,
And her lips grew warm with my name,
And we saw Love's star arise.

Sometimes I but held her hand,
And never a word said we —
We could always understand
With never a word, you see.

Sometimes she chattered like mad,
And laughed — I can hear her now.
Shall I ever again be glad?
I think I've forgotten how.

It is only the name on a door,
Where I used to come and go;
But never to knock there more —
Why, the world seems dead, you know!

VAIN WAITING

The western sky has begun to darken,
The sun has set, and the wind is low;
And waiting alone I sit and hearken
As I used to hearken, ages ago,

For a voice that now the winds know only —

The winds, and the stars, and the vacant night
A presence that vanished and left me lonely,
Reft of all that was heart's delight.

I wait and listen — no step draws nigh me;
Full your world is — empty is mine;
Only the mocking wind sweeps by me,
And flings me never a word or a sign.

A WISH

I wish thee length of days
Filled full of all that's best-
Long years to earn thy bays,
Then twilight time for rest.

I wish thee love and joy —
Love that is strong and sweet —
Gladness without alloy;
A heart with thine to beat.

And then, when Earth has given
Her best and most to thee,
At last I wish thee Heaven —
Then come again to me!

THE COSTLIEST GIFT

I give you a day of my life —
Treasure no gold could buy —
For peasant and peer are at one
When the time comes to die;
And all that the monarch has,
His koh-i-noor or his crown,
He would give for one more day
Ere he lay his dear life down.

They are winged, like the viewless wind —
These days that come and go —
And we count them, and think of the end,
But the end we cannot know:
The whole world darkens with pain
When a sunset fades in the west —
... I give you a day of my life,

My uttermost gift and my best.

TO HER WHO KNOWS

Because your eyes are blue, your lips are red,
And the soft hair is golden on your head,
And your sweet smiling can make glad the day,
And on your cheeks pink roses have their way,

Should I adore you?

Since other maids have shining golden hair,
And other cheeks the June's pink roses wear,
And other eyes can set the day alight,
And other lips can smile with youth's delight,
Why bow before you?

But if the eyes are blue for me alone,
And if for only me the rose has blown,
And but for me the lips their sweet smile wear,
Then shall you mesh me in your golden hair —
I will adore you.

And as my saint, my soul's one shining star,
That lights my darkness from its throne afar,
As lights the summer moon the waiting sea,
With all I am, and all I strive to be,
I'll bow before you.

IN THE OFFING

A ghostly ship sails on a ghostly sea,
And bears afar an anxious company,
Whose dreams, whose hopes, whose constant longings yearn
For some fair port from which no ships return —
Some quiet haven, undisturbed by strife
Of vexing surges from our storm-vext life —
Wind-driven surges from our wind-swept life.

My longing heart sails with them as they go,
Anxious as they, and heavy with their woe;
Where is the peaceful shore we long to find —
The waves are stormy, and the path is blind —
The distant sky shuts in the distant sea —

What star of promise holds the dark for me?
What star of promise holds the dark for thee?

WITH A BOOK

You fain would know the story of my life?
Nay, then you shall divine it from my song —
The weariness of ever-baffled strife;
The Joy that fled, the Grief that lingers long;

The barren shore, laved by the bitter tide;
The vanity of all beneath the sun;
The longing, that Fate's mockery denied;
The triumph unachieved; the goal unwon;

The fleeting moments, vague and sweet and dear
As violets upon a grave that grow: —
Is not the whole vain story written here?
Then turn these leaves, and you my soul shall know.

SONNETS

A Sonnet is a moment's monument —
Memorial from the Soul's Eternity
To one dead, deathless hour.
D. G. Rossetti.

LOVE'S ROSARY

To unpathed waters, undreamed shores.
Shakespeare.

I.

LAND OF MY DREAMS

O spacious, splendid Land that no man knows,
Whose mystery as the tideless sea is deep,
Whose beauty haunts me in the courts of sleep!
What whispering wind from thy hid garden blows,
Sweet with the breath of Love's celestial rose?

What field hast thou that mortal may not reap?
What soft enchantment do those meadows keep
Through which Life's bright, unfathomed river flows?

I can resist thy charm when noon is high;
Mine ears are deafened while earth's clamors rave;
But now the sun has set, the winds are low,
And Night with her proud company draws nigh,
Thy spell prevails, thy mystic joys I crave —
Land of my Dreams, I will arise and go.

II.

THOUGH WE WERE DUST

In the vast realms of unconjectured space,
Where devious paths eternally outspread,
Where farthest stars their mighty marches tread,
And unknown suns through unknown systems pace,
What power can give our longing hearts the grace
To follow feet that long ago have fled,
Among the thronging populace of the dead
To find the welcome of the one dear face?

Nay! Let the souls throng round us! I am I,
And you are you! We should not vainly seek:
Would you not hear, though faint and far my call?
Nay, were we dust, and had no lips to speak,
Our very atoms on the winds blown by
Would meet, and cling, whatever might befall.

III.

THE ROSE OF DAWN

How mockingly the morning dawns for me,
Since thou art gone where no pursuing speech,
No prayer, no farthest-sounding cry can reach!
I call, and wait the answer to my plea —
But only hear the stern, dividing sea,
That pauses not, however I beseech,
Breaking, and breaking, on the distant beach
Of that far land whereto thy soul did flee.

Do happy suns shine on thee where thou art?
And kind stars cheer with friendly ray thy night?
And strange birds wake with music strange thy morn?
This beggared world, where thou no more hast part,
Misapprehends the morning's young delight,
And the old grief makes the new day forlorn.

IV.

THOU REIGNEST STILL

Thou liv'st and reignest in my memory,
Discrowned of earth, but crowned still in the soul
Subject to thee from pole to utmost pole: —
This is the kingdom thou hast still in fee,
Though Silence and the Night have hidden thee —
King, crowned in joy, and crowned again in dole,
Sovereign and master of my being's whole,
My heart, and life, and all there is of me.

It is thy breath I breathe upon the air;
Thou shinest on me with the stars of night;
Thou risest for me with the morning sun;
I enter Dreamland's Court and find thee there,
And finding quiver with the old delight,
When life and love and hope had just begun.

V.

TIME'S PRISONER

Time was, beloved, when from this far-off place
My words could reach thee, and thine own reply —
Now thou art gone, and ray heart's longing cry
Pursues thee, as some runner runs his race —
Cleaves like a bird the emptiness of space,
And falls back, baffled, from the pitiless sky.
Ah, why with thee, so dear, did I not die?
Why should I live benighted of thy face?

Thou wilt have sped so far before I come —
How shall I ever win to where thou art?
Or, if I find thee, shall I not be dumb —
With voiceless longing break my silent heart?
Nay! Surely thou wilt read mine eyes, and know
That for thy sake all heaven I would forego.

VI

HAVE I NOT LEARNED TO LIVE WITHOUT THEE YET?

Have I not learned to live without thee yet? —
Years joined to scornful years have mocked my pain;
Light-footed joys have proffered transient gain,
And smiled on me, and wooed me to forget;
And lesser loves my pathway have beset
With cheap enticements. Since my heart was fain,
Sometimes I listened, but their boast was vain, —
They had no coin to pay the old time's debt.

And thou? Thou art at rest, and far away
From all the vain delusions of the hour;
Like some forsaken child, I weep by night,
While thou rejoicest in thy perfect day:
Thine is the triumph, thine the immortal power, —
Art thou too glad to mourn for earth's delight?

VII.

A HEAVENLY BIRTHDAY

Dost thou take note and say, in thy far place,
"This birthday is the first since that dark hour
When on my breast was laid Love's funeral flower?"
Thou hast won all, in the immortal race —
Conquerer of life and death and time and space —
And I, a lagging, beaten runner, cower,
While round me mocking memories jeer and lower,
And from thy far world comes no helpful grace.

Thou dost not whisper that those heights are cold
Where I walk not beside thee, and the night
Of death is long. Nay, I am over-bold!
Thou sittest comforted and healed with light,
And young and glad; and I who wait am old;
Yet shall I find thee, even in Death's despite.

VIII.

LETHE

What shall assuage the unforgotten pain,
And teach the unforgetful to forget?
D. G. ROSSBTTI.

I tire of phantoms that my heart distrain,
That claim their own, and will not let me rest,
That mock me with old laughter, long-hushed jest,
And of the love I promised once are fain.
Shall I not seek some opiate for pain,
And drug the ceaseless ache within my breast —
Bid Memory "Hence!" as an unwelcome guest,
And smite the joyous chords of life again?

Nay! Then must I forbid the dead to speak,
And do the holy past unholy wrong —
Disown its claim — refuse to pay its debt —
All Heaven would look with scorn on one so weak!
I choose, instead, to suffer and be strong —
Give me no Lethe! I will not forget

IX.

A SILENT VOICE

They bid me welcome in the proud New Year,
Crowned with delight, his Minister the Sun —
Monarch, whose sumptuous reign has just begun:
Nay, I am deaf — their shouts I do not hear —
I miss a voice that long ago was dear;
A tender voice, whose lightest call had won
My ear, my heart, my life, till life were done: —
That voice is silent — theirs I will not hear.

A little bird that finds the winter cold
Comes out, and looks at me, and sings of him
Who made the vanished summers warm; and, bold
With sorrow, calls the New Year's splendor dim.
Nay, bird, he is gone far who used to sing;
And days, and months, and years no message bring.

X.

WERE BUT MY SPIRIT LOOSED UPON THE AIR

Were but my spirit loosed upon the air —
By some High Power who could Life's chains unbind,

Set free to seek what most it longs to find —
To no proud Court of Kings would I repair:
I would but climb, once more, a narrow stair,
When day was wearing late, and dusk was kind;
And one should greet me to my failings blind,
Content so I but shared his twilight there.

Nay! well I know he waits not as of old —
I could not find him in the old-time place —
I must pursue him, made by sorrow bold,
Through worlds unknown, in strange celestial race,
Whose mystic round no traveller has told,
From star to star, until I see his face.

OF LIFE AND LOVE

The Accumulated Past.
D. G. Rossetti.

AT MIDSUMMER

The spacious Noon enfolds me with its peace —
The affluent Midsummer wraps me round —
So still the earth and air, that scarce a sound
Affronts the silence, and the swift caprice
Of one stray bird's lone call does but increase
The sense of some compelling hush profound,
Some spell by which the whole vast world is bound,
Till star-crowned Night smile downward its release.

I sit and dream — midway of the long day —
Midway of the glad year — midway of life —
My whole world seems, indeed, to hold its breath: —
For me the sun stands still upon his way —
The winds for one glad hour remit their strife —
Then Day, and Year, and Life whirl on toward Death.

THE LIFE-MASK OF KEATS*

Poet to poet gave this mask, of him
Who sang the song of Rapture and Despair;
Who to the Nightingale was kin; aware

Of all the Night's enamouring — the dim
Strange ecstasy of light at the moon's rim;
The unheard melodies that subtly snare
The listening soul — Pan's wayward pipes that dare
To conjure shapes now beautiful, now grim.

He who this life-mask prized so tenderly
Might not behold the semblance that it wore,
The charm ineffable — now sweet, now sad:
But well he knew what loveliness must be
Upon the face of Keats for evermore,
And with his spirit's gaze saw and was glad.

Given to the blind poet, Philip Bourke Marston, by Richard Watson Gilder.

SOUL TO BODY

Oh, long-time Friend, 'tis many a year since we
Took hands together, and came through the morn,
When thou and day and I were newly born —
And fair the future looked, and glad and free —
A year as long as whole Eternity —
And full of roses with no stinging thorn,
And full of joys that could not be outworn;
And time was measureless for thee and me.

Long have we fared together, thou and I:
Thou hast grown dearer, as old friends must grow:
Small wonder if I dread to say good-by
When our long pact is over, and I go
To enter strange, new worlds beyond the sky,
Called by that Power to whom no man saith No.

AT REST

Shall I lie down to sleep, and see no more
The splendid pageantry of earth and sky —
The proud procession of the stars sweep by;
The white moon sway the sea, and woo the shore;
The morning lark to the far Heaven soar;
The nightingale with the soft dusk draw nigh;
The summer roses bud, and bloom, and die —
Will Life and Life's delight for me be o'er?

Nay! I shall be, in my low silent home,
Of all Earth's gracious ministries aware —
Glad with the gladness of the risen day,
Or gently sad with sadness of the gloam,
Yet done with striving, and foreclosed of care —
At rest — at rest! What better thing to say?

SHALL I COMPLAIN?

Shall I complain because the feast is o'er,
And all the banquet lights have ceased to shine?
For joy that was, and is no longer mine;
For love that came and went, and comes no more;
For hopes and dreams that left my open door;
Shall I, who hold the past in fee, repine? . . .
Nay! there are those who never quaffed life's wine —
That were the unblest fate one might deplore.

To sit alone and dream, at set of sun,
When all the world is vague with coming night —
To hear old voices whisper, sweet and low,
And see dear faces steal back, one by one,
And thrill anew to each long-past delight —
Shall I complain, who still this bliss may know?

PARTING

"Tis you, not I, have chosen. Love, go free!
No cry of mine shall hold you on your way.
I wept above the dead Past yesterday: —
Let it lie now where all fair dead things be,
Beneath the waves of Time's all-whelming sea.
Forget it or remember — come what may —
The time is past when one could bid it stay:
What boots it any more to you or me?

It was my life — what matter? — I am dead,
And if I seem to move, or speak, or smile,
If some strange round of being still I tread
And am not buried, for a little while,
Yet, look you, Love, I am not what I seem:
I died when died my faith in that dear dream.

VAIN FREEDOM

So I am free whom Love held thrall so long!
Now will I flaunt my colors on the air,
And with triumphal music scale heaven's stair,
Till all those shining choirs shall hush their song,
And hark in silent wonder to the strong,
Compelling harmonies that boldly dare
To soar so high, and make the blest aware
That, free like them, I stand their ranks among.

Nay! but my triumph mocks me, — chills the day:
Bound would I be, and suffer, and be sad,
Rather than free, and with no heart to ache.
Strong God of Love, still hold me in thy sway!
Give back my human pain; let me go mad
With the old dreams, old tortures, for Love's sake.

THE NEW YEAR DAWNS

The New Year dawns — the sun shines strong and clear;
And all the world rejoices and is gay;
The city-loving birds from spray to spray
Flit busily and twitter in my ear
Their little frozen note of wintry cheer:
From ruddy children with the snow at play
Ring peals of laughter gladder than in May,
While friend greets friend, with "Happy be thy Year!"

So would I joy, if Thou wert by my side —
So would I laugh, if Thou couldst laugh with me —
But, left alone, in Darkness I abide,
Mocked by a Day that shines no more on thee:
From this too merry world my heart I hide —
My New Year dawns not till thy face I see.

ASPIRATION

Break, ties that bind me to this world of sense,
Break, now, and loose me on the upper air: —
Those skies are blue; and that far dome is fair
With prophecy of some divine, intense,
Undreamed-of rapture. Ah, from thence

I catch a music that my soul would snare
With its strange sweetness; and I seem aware
Of Life that waits to crown this life's suspense.

I see — I hear — yet to this world I cling —
This fatal world of passion and unrest —
Where loss and pain jeer at each human bliss,
As autumn mocks the fleetness of the spring,
And each morn sees its sunset in the west —
Break, ties that bind me to a world like this 1

OH, TRAVELLER BY UNACCUSTOMED WAYS

Oh, traveller by unaccustomed ways —
Searcher among new worlds for pleasures new —
Art thou content because the skies are blue,
And blithe birds thrill the air with roundelays,
And the fair fields with sunshine are ablaze?
Dost thou not find thy heart's-ease twined with rue,
And long for some dear bloom on earth that grew —
Some wild, sweet fragrance of remembered days?

I send my message to thee by the stars —
Since other messenger I may not find
Till I go forth beyond these prisoning bars,:
Leaving this memory-haunted world behind,
To seek thee, claim thee, wheresoe'er thou be,
Since Heaven itself were empty, lacking thee.

GREAT LOVE

I.

GREAT LOVE IS HUMBLE

Humble is Love, for he is Honor's child:
He knows the worth of her he does adore,
And that high reckoning humbles him the more:
By her dear sweetness from his pain beguiled,
He would be proud because her look is mild;
But all the while he scans the oft-told score,
And his imperfectness must still deplore,
Abashed no less because on him she smiled.

To be allowed to love is Love's dear prize:
To lay his homage at Her royal feet —
To enter thus the true heart's paradise,
The name of names forever to repeat,
And read his sentence in her answering eyes —
Love should be humble — his reward is meet.

II.

GREAT LOVE IS PROUD

For very humbleness Great Love is proud:
The round world were a tribute thrice too small
To render to the rightful queen of all —
Yet why should Love's least gift be disavowed —
If once her royal head the queen has bowed,
Lending her gracious ear to the low call
Of him whose glory is to be her thrall —
Who only prays his worship be allowed?

Once to have known her fairness — who is fair
Beyond the dreamer's dream, the painter's art —
This, only this, were bliss above compare:
But if he find the gateway to her heart,
Shall he not, like a king, be set apart
Who for one royal moment entered there?

HER YEARS

Years come and go, each bringing in his train,
Spring fair with promise, Summer glad with bloom,
Fruit-bearing Autumn, and the Winter's gloom;
But years and seasons march for Her in vain,
Since still she strings her rosary of pain,
Catching from far some subtle, lost perfume,
Some scent of roses dying on a tomb,
Unfreshened by Spring's dew or Summer's rain.

Why change the seasons when She cannot change?
For pomp of morn, high noon, or setting sun
What cares she? They are powerless to estrange
Her soul from Grief, who, till her day is done,
Companions her wherever she may range,
And makes her New Years old, ere yet begun.

MIDWINTER FLOWERS

TO E. C. S.

I hold you to my lips and heart, fair flowers,
Dear, first-begotten children of the sun —
Whose summer lives in winter were begun;
Sweet aliens from the warm June's pleasant bowers,
Mocked at by cruel winds in desolate hours
Through which the sands of winter slowly run:
I touch your tender petals, one by one,
And miss no beauty born of summer showers.

I have a friend who to Life's winter days
Will bring the warmth and splendor of the June;
From him ye come, yet need not speak his praise,
Since on my heart is written well that rune,
And the fine fragrance of his gentle deeds
Reveals his presence 'mong earth's common weeds.

HER PRESENCE

I long in vain by day, but when the night
With all its jewels stars the waiting sky,
And vagrant fireflies like stray souls flit by,
She seeks me in the tender waning light,
And sits beside me there, a Presence white; —
Her eyes yearn for me, and her dear lips sigh,
But if to clasp her cold soft hands I try
The shadows deepen, and she fades from sight.

O lost and dear! — by what strange, devious way
Does she escape? for I, too, fain would flee
From all the hollow pageantry of life,
And with her through immortal meadows stray.
The free winds mock my quest, stars laugh to see,
And I wait helpless till Death end the strife.

WHEN WE CONFRONT THE VASTNESS OF THE NIGHT

When we confront the Vastness of the Night,
And meet the gaze of her eternal eyes,

How trivial seem the garnered gains we prize —
The laurel wreath we flaunt to envious sight;
The flower of Love we pluck for our delight;
The mad, sweet music of the heart, that cries
An instant on the listening air, then dies —
How short the day of all things dear and bright!

The Everlasting mocks our transient strife;
The pageant of the Universe whirls by
This little sphere with petty turmoil rife —
Swift as a dream and fleeting as a sigh —
This brief delusion that we call our life,
Where all we can accomplish is to die.

ON MEETING A SAILING VESSEL IN MID-OCEAN

She moves on grandly 'twixt the sea and sky,
Like some gigantic bird from foreign shore;
Gray mist behind her and gray mist before,
Riding upon the waters royally.
Salt winds caress her, as they urge her by,
And we who watch shall see her nevermore;
For on she goes, to where the breakers roar
Round some far coast we never may descry.

So on Life's tide we meet an unknown soul,
And catch a passing vision of its grace;
Just seen, then vanished, leaving us to yearn
With vain desire to follow to its goal
The revelation of the radiant face —
Then heartsick to our solitude we turn.

MIDNIGHT AT SEA

Through the deep stillness of the awful night,
I heard the clamor of the ship's great bell —
A voice cried: "Twelve o'clock, and all is well!"
Then silence, and the solemn, watching light
Of the white moon, on billows wild and white
That yielded, to her magical, dear spell,
The stormy hearts no lesser charm could quell —
Slaves of her lamp, and powerless to affright.

Ah, when across the wide, unfathomed sea

Which no chart maps, whose depth no plummet knows,
To some dim, unconjectured shore we steer,
Through that wild night, into whose depths we flee
Farther than any wind from this world blows,
May cry of "All is well" our midnight cheer!

INTER MANES

In the dim watches of the midmost night,
A ghost confronts him, standing by his bed,
A lonesome ghost who walks uncomforted,
Pale child of Memory and dead Delight,
No longer fair or pleasant in his sight.
With dusky hair upon her shoulders shed,
And cypress leaves for garland on her head,
As patient as the moonlight and as white,
She stands beside him, and puts forth her hand
To lead him backward into Love's lost Land —
Sad Land which shadows people, and where wait
Memory, her sire, and dead Delight, his mate —
And standing there among the shadowy band,
He learns how Love mocks him who loves too late.

YET, STRANGELY BEAUTIFUL YOUR FACE I FIND

Yet, strangely beautiful your face I find;
Your voice is like the murmur that decrees
A morn of April, and awakes the trees
To meet the soft caresses of the wind.
Like sudden light your presence makes us blind;
From your compelling spell the weak man flees,
The strong man sues you on his bended knees;
And with your golden hair their chains you bind.

I am not of them. Not to you I kneel.
Cold is your charm — like the white moon your soul;
For something more akin to me I yearn.
You can enthrall; but, Empress, can you feel?
March on, unchallenged, to your far-off goal;
From you to some more human heart I turn.

A SUMMER'S DREAM

I.

What that dead summer was my heart knows well —
Knows all it held — sad joy, and joyous pain —
For pain or joy it cannot come again,
With bitter sweetness we alone could tell: —
Time, when I only thought to say farewell,
To break the links of Love's long-during chain —
That I the stars should pass, and you remain,
Held fast to earth by some malignant spell.

Procession of long days, and longer nights —
When suns rose mocking, and the moon was cold —
When Hope and I lay dying, as I thought,
Still could I bless Love's vanishing delights,
And reach pale hands to clasp him as of old,
Though each dread hour with Death's dismay was fraught.

II.

So Summer, with her slow, reluctant feet,
Went by, and lingering smiled, as loth to part,
While fond delusions warmed my lonesome heart: —
Though lives were severed, winged dreams could meet;
So met we, dear, as bodiless spirits greet —
Met, and were blind, foreseeing not the smart
Of hopes that hope not, and of tears that start
From eyes that say what lips may not repeat.

One brief day here, then gone beyond the sun —
How short the way, how soon the goal is won —
So less or more of love why need we measure?
But Fate avenges pleasant things begun,
And Retribution spares not any one,
And no Gods pity those who steal their treasure.

MY MASTERS

The first of all my masters was Delight —
I bent my knee to worship him, and sought
His ministers, and all the bliss they wrought,
In Day's large splendor, and the peace of Night,
In song, and mirth, and every goodly sight;
Until fair Love another lesson taught,

And bitter pain dearer than pleasure brought,
And my whole soul was subject to his might.

Brief while I strove for Fame — his laurel wreath
Seemed good to wear, and dear the fleeting breath
With which men praise the idol of an hour;
But one drew nigh me clothed upon with power,
And looking in the awful eyes of Death
I knew the Master at whose touch we cower.

TO PRINCE ORIC

(SIX YEARS OLD)

Do you remember, centuries gone by,
When you were king, and I, your subject, came
To kiss your hand, and swell the loud acclaim
Wherewith the people greeted you, and cry —
"Long life, and love, and glory, O most high
And puissant lord"? The city was aflame
With torches; banners streamed; and knight and dame
Knelt at your feet — you smiled your proud reply.

I think you do remember; for I caught
That same elusive smile upon your lips,
When ended was the centuries' eclipse,
And I, my sovereign found, my homage brought:
"Long life, and love, and glory, now as then!"
And you? — your smile is my reward again.

A POETS SECOND LOVE

I.

I share your heart with her, its former Queen,
Who taught your lips the song of love to sing —
To whose high altar you were wont to bring
Such laurels as no Fair since Time hath been
Has decked her brow with. Joy was there and teen.
And reverence, as for some most sacred thing
Set high in Heaven for all men's worshipping \
Such laurels gathers no man twice, I ween.

Your second love, ungarlanded, uncrowned —

Fit for life's daily uses, let us say —
Whose lips have never thrilled you with sweet sound,
Hears from the grave your first love's voice, to-day.
With scornful laughter mock her hope to fill
The heart ruled by its earliest sovereign still.

II.

Not mine the spell to charm your lute to song;
A poet you, yet not for me your lays;
You crowned that other woman with your praise,
Lifting your voice to Heaven, triumphant, strong,
And later rhymes might do her laurels wrong;
Should you and I together tread life's ways,
An echo would pursue us from old days,
And men would say — " He loved once, well and long,
So now without great love he is content,
Since she is dead whose praise he used to sing,
And daily needs demand their aliment." . . .
Thus some poor bird, who strives with broken wing
To soar, might stoop — strength gone and glad life spent —
To any hand that his scant food would bring.

FAIR LIFE

Fair Life, thou dear companion of my days —
Life with the rose-red lips and shining eyes —
That led'st me through my Youth's glad Paradise,
And stand'st beside me still, in these dull ways
My older feet must tread, the tangled maze
Where cares beset me and fresh foes surprise;
On the keen wind and from the far-off skies
Is borne a whisper, which my heart dismays,
That thou and I must part. Beloved so long,
Wilt thou not stay with me, inconstant Love?
Nay, then, the cry upon the wind grows strong —
I must without thee fresh adventure prove;
And yet it may be I but do thee wrong,
And I shall find thee waiting where I rove.

A PLEA FOR THE OLD YEAR

I see the smiling New Year climb the heights —

The clouds, his heralds, turn the sky to rose,
And flush the whiteness of the winter snows
Till Earth is glad with Life and Life's delight.
The weary Old Year died when died the night,
And this new comer, proud with triumph, shows
His radiant face, and each glad subject knows
The welcome Monarch, born to rule aright.

Yet there are graves far-off that no man tends,
Where lie the vanished loves and hopes and fears,
The dreams that grew to be our hearts' best friends,
The smiles, and, dearer than the smiles, the tears —
These were that Old Year's gifts, whom none defends,
Now his strong Conqueror, the New, appears.

WHEN I AM DEAD

When I am dead and buried underground,
And your dear eyes still greet the shining day,
Will you remember — "Thus she used to say —
And thus, and thus, her low voice used to sound"?
Will memory wander like a ghost around
The well-known paths — tread the accustomed way;
Or will you pluck fresh blossoms of the May,
And waste no rose upon my burial mound?

I would not have your life to sorrow wed —
Your joyous youth grief-stricken for my sake; —
Though black-winged Care her home with you should make,
Yet vain would be the scalding tears you shed;
And though your heart for love of me should break,
How could I hear, or heed, if I were dead?

ONE AFTERNOON

TO LOUISA, LADY ASHBURTON

From the dear stillness of your pines you came —
That vast Cathedral where the winds are choir,
And bear to the far heavens the soul's desire,
While the great sun burns golden, like the flame,
On some high altar, to the Highest Name —
From that dear shrine whence worldly thoughts retire —
Where hearts are hushed, and souls to Heaven aspire,

You came, as one who would God's peace proclaim.

Now sunset broods upon these solemn hills —
The day is done, and the deep night draws nigh,
And soon the waiting stars will light the sky: —
Though You and Day have gone, your presence fills
The place, and the glad air around me thrills
As if some Heaven-sent angel had passed by.

IN QUEST OF NIGHT

Darkness surrounds us.
William Wordsworth.

Once in a dream I saw the flowers
That bud and bloom in Paradise.
Christina Rossetti.

AFAR FROM GOD

Fain would I scale the heights that lead to God,
But my feet stumble and my steps are weak,
Warm are the valleys, and the hills are bleak:
Here, where I linger, flowers make soft the sod,
But those far paths that martyr feet have trod
Are sharp with flints, and from their farthest peak
The still, small voice but faintly seems to speak,
While here the drowsy lilies dream and nod.

I have dreamed with them, till the night draws nigh
In which I cannot climb: still high above,
In the blue vastness of the awful sky,
Those unsealed heights my fatal weakness prove —
Those shining heights which I must reach, or die
Afar from God, unquickened by His love.

MY FATHER'S HOUSE

When shall I join the blessed company
Of those this barren world to me denies?
When shall I wake to the new day's surprise,
Beyond the murmur of death's moaning sea,

In that glad home where my best loved ones be;
And know that I have found my Paradise,
Finding again the love that never dies
The heart's dear welcome, biding there for me?

I wait alone upon life's wind-swept beach —
The waves are high — the sea is wild and wide —
Yet Death, bold pilot, all their wrath shall dare,
And guide me to the shore I fain would reach: —
Even now I hear the swift, incoming tide,
Whose slow, eternal ebb my bark shall bear.

NEWLY BORN

Out of the dark into the arms of love
The babe is born, and recks not of the way
His soul has traversed to confront the day:
Enough for him the face that smiles above,
The tireless feet that on his errands move,
The arms that clasp, the tender lips that kiss,
The whole dear wealth of welcome and of bliss
His heirship and his sovereignty that prove.

So may there be no place for Earth's vain tears
When Heaven's great rapture bursts upon the sight: —
Shall not the soul, new-born in heavenly spheres,
Forget the paths it traversed, and the night
It journeyed through, and all old hopes and fears,
Caught up into that Infinite, Great Light?

THE SONG OF THE STARS

In those high heavens wherein the fair stars flower,
They do God's praises sound from night till morn,
And till the smiling day is newly born
Chant each to each His glory and His power;
Then, silent, wait, through Day's brief triumph-hour,
Watching till Night shall come again, with scorn
Of those chameleon splendors that adorn
Day's death, and then before his victor cower.

Forever, to immortal ears, they sing, —
These shining stars that praise their Maker's grace —
And from far world to world their anthems ring:

They shine and sing because they see His face
We, cowards, dread the vision Death shall bring,
The waking rapture, and the fair, far place.

A QUESTION: AT SEA

How dark the clouds that hide the sky from sight,
While winds like human souls moan round our keel,
Their woe inexplicable to reveal —
With lone, unsilenced cries for lost delight,
That suns by day, or journeying moons by night
Can find no more, till the vast heavens reel
And the strong worlds are rent by that last peal,
The trumpet-blast that puts old Time to flight.

Then, when the End has come, and Chaos reigns,
And darkness mocks past glories of the sun,
Will human hearts forget their human pains
In some unearthly blessedness, new- won?
Shall we outlast this brief earth's transient gains,
And know ourselves the one thing not undone?

THE LAND OF GOLD

Behind the sunset's bars in the wide West,
We catch the radiance of the Land of Gold;
The dazzling splendors of its wealth untold
Flash through our dreams, and wake to vague unrest
The soul — with Life's dull weariness opprest,
Or wrapped in weeds of sorrow, fold on fold —
Till, with sheer longing and despair grown bold,
We turn to seek that Land where all are blest.

But the Gold fades, and the strong stars arise
That look beyond the sunset and the sun;
They see our little world swing far below,
While over it imperial planets glow —
From Heaven they whisper, "Heaven cannot be won
Until great Death has come to make men wise."

A PRAYER IN THE DARK

I stretch my hand out through the lonesome night,
My helpless hand, and pray Thee, Lord, to lead
My ignorant steps, and help me at my need:
Far off from home, pity my hapless plight,
And through the darkness guide me on to light!
I have no hope unless my cry Thou heed, —
Be merciful; for I am lost, indeed,
Unless thy rising sun the darkness smite.

How shall I find, who know not how to seek?
Kindle my soul, enlighten my dull mind;
My heart is heavy, and my faith is weak, —
A stone am I, and deaf and dumb and blind, —
Unhelped of Thee my footsteps helpless stray, —
Have pity, Thou, and lead me to the Day!

AT DEATH's POSTERN

The dead but sceptered sovereigns who still rule.
Byron.

The ways of Death are soothing and serene -—
And all the words of Death are grave and sweet.
W. E. Henley.

ACROSS THE SEA

Into the silence of the silent night
He passed, whom all men honor; and the sun
Arose to shine upon a world undone,
And barren lives, bereft of Life's delight.
The morning air was chill with sudden blight,
And Winter's cruel triumph had begun;
But He to some far Summer shore had won,
Whose splendor hides him from our dazzled sight.

Not England's pride alone, this Lord of Song!
We — heirs to Shakespeare's and to Milton's speech —
Claim heritage from Tennyson's proud years:
To us his spacious, splendid lines belong —
We, too, repeat his praises, each to each —
We share his glory, and we share your tears.

October, 1892.

ROBERT BROWNING

I.

HIS STAR

The Century was young — the month was May—
The spacious East was kindled with a light
That lent a sudden glory to the night,
And a new star began its upward way
Toward the high splendor of the perfect day:
With pure white flame, inexorably bright,
It reached the souls of men — no stain so slight
As to escape its all-revealing ray.

When countless voices cried, "The Star has set!"
And through the lands there surged a sea of pain,
Was it Death's triumph — victory of Woe? —
Nay! There are lights the sky may not forget:
When suns, and moons, and souls shall rise again,
In the New Life's wide East that star shall glow.

ROBERT BROWNING

II.

THE POET OF HUMAN LIFE

Silence and Night sequestered thee in vain!
Oblivion's threats thou proudly couldst defy.
Thou art not dead — such great souls do not die:
One small world's range no longer could constrain
That strong-winged spirit of its freedom fain:
New stars, new lives, thy fearless quest would try.
Our baffled vision may not soar so high —
We mourn, as loss, thine infinite, great gain.

Yet, keen of sight, to whom men's souls lay bare,
Stripped clean of shams, unclothed of all disguise,
Revealed to thee as if at each soul's birth
Thou hadst been nigh to stamp it foul or fair —
Why shouldst thou seek new schools to make thee wise
Who shared Heaven's secrets whilst thou walked on earth?

December, 1890.

And can it be on the relentless blast
The Last Leaf has blown by — the tree is bare?
Strange was the chill that shivered on the air,
As if an unclothed soul were hurrying past,
In search of some new region strange and vast —
Some Country unexplored, where dead men fare,
Assuaged of Life, and all Life's carking care,
To the Great Rapture, waiting them at last.

He may be glad for whom the Heavens ope,
And the New Day shines royally and clear —
But we, who mourn him and shall mourn him long,
For what meet consolation shall we hope —
Or whither shall our sorrow turn for cheer,
Bereft of our dear Singer, and his song?

October, 1894.

SUMMONED BY THE KING*

He was at home in Courts and knew the great,
Himself was of them. Ofttimes Kings have sent
To call him to their presence; and he went,
A welcome guest, to share their royal state,
For earth's high potentates a fitting mate.
He was of all men honored — crowned of Song,
And crowned of Love — and high above the wrong
Of envy, or the littleness of hate.

And now the mightiest King — to summon him
To that far place whereto all souls must come —
Has sent swift Azrael, Heaven's chamberlain, —
Beyond the ultimate sea's remotest rim,
Where all the voices of this earth are dumb,
The Courtier journeys — called to Court again.

*James Russell Lowell — August, 1891.

PHILIP BOURKE MARSTON

AUTHOR OF "GARDEN SECRETS

He, who those secrets whispered — he is dead —
No more the rose and lily shall confide
To him how faithless was the Wind that sighed
With fleeting love, rifled their bloom and fled;
The "Garden Fairies," by Titania led,
Ring no more chimes of rapture since he died;
And from unseen "Wind Gardens," where abide
The souls of blossoms, no sweet breath is shed.

His flowers and he have vanished: yet, who knows
Through what fair fields unwitnessed of the sun
He wanders, among blossoms red and white,
Fostered of Joy — where never chill blast blows,
And the glad year is always just begun? —
Nor Time, nor Death, immortal youth can blight.

THE CLOSED GATE

But life is short; so gently close the gate.
Winifred Howells.

Thus wrote she when the heart in her was high,
And her brief tale of youth seemed just begun.
Like some white flower that shivers in the sun
She heard from far the low winds prophesy —
Blowing across the grave where she must lie —
Had strange prevision of the victory won
In the swift race that Life with Death should run,
And, hand in hand with Life, saw Death draw nigh.

Beyond this world the hostile surges foam:
Our eyes are dim with tears and cannot see
In what fair paths her feet our coming wait,
What stars rise for her in her far new home: —
We but conjecture all she yet may be,
While on the Joy she was, we close the gate.

A DREAM IN THE NIGHT

TO MY MOTHER

Sometimes it seems thy face — thy long-hid face —
Looks out on me as from a passing cloud,
Till I forget they clad thee in thy shroud.
And laid thee sleeping in thy far-off place —
So once again the tender, healing grace
Of thy dear presence is to me allowed.
Wilt thou not bless the head before thee bowed?
Wilt not thy voice thrill through the empty space?

How lone and cold the world without thee seemed I
Regaining thee, how warm it is and bright!
Yet all in vain to reach thee do I seek: —
And then I wake to know I have but dreamed,
And thou art silent as the silent night —
With tears I call thee, yet thou dost not speak.

RONDELS AND RONDEAUR

With pipe and flute the rustic Pan
Of old made music sweet for man.
Austin Dobson,

Like echo of an old refrain
That long within the mind has lain.
Canon Bell.

VAGRANT LOVE

O vagrant Love! do you come this way?
I hear you knock at the long- closed door
That turned too oft on its hinge before —
I am stronger now; I can say you Nay.

The vague, sweet smile on your lips to-day,
Its meaning and magic I know of yore:
O vagrant Love, do you come this way?
I hear your knock at the long- closed door.

But why your summons should I obey?
I listened once till my heart grew sore —
Shall I listen again, and again deplore?
Nay! Autumn must ever be wiser than May —

And the more we welcome the more you betray —
O vagrant Love, would you come this way?

THOUGH WE REPENT

Though we repent, can any God give back
The dear, lost days we might have made so fair —
Turn false to true, and carelessness to care
And let us find again what now we lack?

Oh, once, once more to tread the old-time track,
The flowers we threw away once more to wear —
Though we repent, can any God give back
The dear, lost days we might have made so fair?

Who can repulse a stealthy ghost's attack —
Silence a voice that doth the midnight dare —
Make fresh hopes spring from grave-sod of despair —

Set free a tortured soul from memory's rack?
Though we repent, can any God give back
The dear, lost days we might have made so fair?

THE SPRING IS HERE

I feel the kindness of the lengthening days —
I warm me at the strong fire of the sun —
I know the year's glad course is well begun —
Ah, what awaits me in its devious ways?

What strange, new bliss shall thrill me with amaze?
What prize shall I rejoice that I have won?
I feel the kindness of the lengthening days —
I warm me at the strong fire of the sun.

Yet I behold the phantom that dismays —
The face of Grief that spares not any one —
Rewards come not until the task is done,
And there are minor chords in all earth's lays; —
Nay! Trust the kindness of the lengthening days —
I 'll warm me at the strong fires of the sun.

TO THE GHOST OF MARY QUEEN OF SCOTS

Fair, ruthless Ghost, I know you well!
High poets praised you with their lays,
Yet could not half your beauty tell;
So, now, your loveliness dismays

My rhyme, and mocks my poor essays
To hint, in words, its magic spell.
Ah, witching Queen, strange woes befell
The bards who served you in old days!

Sweet, ruthless Ghost, their songs of praise
Like warning music with me dwell,
And bid me to beware your plays
With love and death — your charm repel.
You smile again! that smile betrays
Hearts still are playthings: Fare you well.

AFTER SUPPING WITH A POET

TO E. G.

You called your mystic draught Canary sack —
I drank, and dreamed of far-off Southern seas,
And heard the wraiths of vagrant melodies;
And Joys and Hopes from some dim shade came back.

What blithe feet walked upon a grass-grown track!
What glad winds gossiped under summer trees!
You called your mystic draught Canary sack —
I drank, and dreamed of far-off Southern Seas.

This wine, from strange grapes pressed, upon my track
Lets loose the band of Ancient Memories:
Now this sole cup my waywardness can please;
All other brews some fine distinction lack —
You called your magic draught Canary sack!

ROSAMOND'S ROSE

Rosamond gave me a rose,
Rose-red and alive in the sun:
Ah, what was its secret? Who knows? —

Her garden held only that one.

Now alive in my heart it glows;
By its magic my peace is undone —
There are spells that the wise should shun
Rosamond gave me a rose.

But where is my old repose?
She calls — to her feet I run:
Oh, who shall the secret disclose?
Or how was my bondage begun? —
Rosamond gave me a rose,
Rose-red and alive in the sun.

TO A FAIR LADY

Fair Lady, you were clad in white
When first your gentle eyes I met,
And never shall my heart forget
The vision of that August night.

With the pale moon's transcendent light,
You shone, in your clear heaven set;
Fair Lady, you were clad in white
When first your gentle eyes I met.

Bend, Moon of Women, from your height,
Soothe with your smile earth's care and fret,
Let us be happy in your debt,
Since you Love's varied charms unite;
Your soul and you were clad in white
When first your gentle eyes I met.

TWO THRUSHES MET

FOR M. E. S.

Two thrushes met upon an April day,
And sang a simple song of love and glee:
. . . "And I am I, dear heart, and you are she
Whose tender note beguiled me on my way!"

They did not heed that all the sky was gray,
And not a neighbor leaf on any tree —

Two thrushes met upon an April day,
And sang a simple song of love and glee.

They did not miss the brightness of the May,
Or long the Summer's lavish wealth to see.
"April," he chirped, "is fair enough for me,
And when you sing, lo, Spring is on the way " —
Two thrushes met upon an April day,
And sang a simple song of love and glee.

LOVE MAKES THE SPRING

Has Spring come back? Is this the May
That makes the air so bland to-day?
The wild sweet winds are glad to know —
The waiting flowers begin to blow,
Green things are blithe along the way.

"What happy spell," I hear them say,
"Has turned the Winter into May?"
Each to the other — "Do you know?
Has Spring come back?"

Ah, Love is he who warms the day,
And turns the Winter into May —
And happy things begin to grow,
Alive with Love's glad overflow,
And answer to his ardent ray —
"Spring has come back."

LIFE'S DAY

TO ONE WHO ASKS ME FOR A MERRY SONG

Oh, could I know how long Life's day —
How near its end, or far away —
What space for mirth, what room for tears
Then might I put aside my fears,
And for a little while be gay.

But now, I think, Death soon may stray
Hereward, and find me at my play,
And mock my laughter with his jeers —
Ah, could I know!

And so I tremble 'neath the sway
Of that arch Foe, who at me peers,
And hour by hour my covert nears,
Yet mocks me when I bid him say
How long for me may be Life's day.

QUATRAINS

Sudden and swift, and like a passing wind.
Matthew Arnold.

THE LOST ROOM

When I came out of the fair House of Youth
I heedlessly behind me closed the door —
Now every hour is bitter with the truth
That I can find that portal never more.

AUTUMN DAYS

Autumn days no solace bring
Harvest time is vain —
Come again, O joy of spring —
Come Youth's April pain.

A DEAD POET

She was the brightest thing beneath the sun
Joy had of her his will —
And, now her singing life is spent and done,
The world, seems strange and chill.

IN A LIBRARY

The living ofttimes vex us —
The wise old dead are best —
When Life's vain games perplex us

'T is here we turn for rest

THE KING DETHRONED

He wore the purple a year and a day —
His pride was high, and his will was strong: -
"Then why was his reign so brief?" you say —
He reigneth gently who reigneth long.

WHO KNOWS?

The Lily lifts to mine her nun-like face,
But my wild heart is beating for the Rose:
How can I pause to heed the Lily's grace? —
Shall I repent me by and by? Who knows?

DAY'S MOCKERY

I heard Love's voice thrill all the waiting Night,
And I arose and followed where he led:
Then Morning mocked me with revealing light —
The great bright world was empty — Love was dead.

THE PRODIGAL

Sad penitent, beloved of God thou art,
Thy wandering feet He welcomes home at night —
More dear than those who never did depart
Is the returning sinner, to His sight.

TRANSLATIONS

Turn over a new leaf.
Dekker.

LONG WEEPING

(From the German of Heine)

I have in a dream been weeping;
Thou wert in thy grave, I dreamed.
I awoke from that bitter dreaming,
And still the hot tears streamed.

I have in a dream been weeping;
I dreamed thou wert gone from me.
I awoke, and awake kept weeping,
Long time and bitterly.

I have in a dream been weeping;
I dreamed that. thou still wert kind.
I awoke, but I weep forever:
My tears have made me blind.

BY MOONLIGHT

(From Heine)

Like dark dreams stand the houses,
Stretched out in lengthened row;
And shrouded close in my mantle
I silently by them go.

The bell of the Cathedral
Chimes midnight from above;
I know, with charms and kisses,
Now waits for me my Love.

The moon is my companion,
Who kindly leadeth me;
At last I reach her dwelling,
And cry out joyfully:

"Old Confidante, I thank thee
That thou hast lit my way!
Shine on, now that I leave thee,
And lend the rest thy ray!

"And should'st thou find a lover,
Who lonely makes his moan,
Give him the same dear comfort
That I, of old, have known."

THROUGH THE DARKNESS

(From Heine)

We travelled alone in the darkness,
Posted the whole night through;
On each other's hearts we rested;
We laughed and jested, too.

But with the dawn of the morning,
My Child, how astonished were we;
For between us Love was sitting,
A passenger blind was he.

THE MIRROR

(From the Provencal of Theodore Aubanel)

Oh long ago she dwelt
In this gay little room —
How shall I find my flower
Here where she used to bloom?
O longing, thirsting eyes,
Pursue the dear surprise:
Mirror, thou know'st her well —
Work thou some magic spell
And bring her back!

Here, when the morn was bright,
She bathed her lovely face,
Her little hands she bathed,
And clad herself with grace.
Between lips glad with song
Her teeth shone, white and strong:
Mirror, thou know'st her well —
Work thou some magic spell
To bring her back!

So innocent, so blithe,
Yet starting at a sound,
She let her long hair's veil
Fall her white shoulders round.
Then from her grandsire's book

Her morning prayer she took:
Mirror, thou know'st her well —
Work thou some magic spell
And bring her back!

Ah, there the book leans now,
Against the sacred palm —
Open, as when she prayed,
Or read some holy psalm!
Surely I hear her feet —
The wind with them is fleet:
Mirror, thou know'st her well —
Hast thou no magic spell
To bring her back?

At high mass or at fete
How fair she was to see!
And I, who should have prayed, —
O Lord, forgive thou me! —
Watched her, as there she knelt;
For prayer her name I spelt;
Mirror, thou know'st her well —
Work me some magic spell
And bring her back!

Here leaned she forth to talk;
Here of her tasks she thought;
For God's love and God's poor
Such patient stitches wrought;
Her swift hands to and fro
Before thee used to go:
Mirror, thou know'st her well,
Yet hast no magic spell
To bring her back!

Glad days of foolish chat,
Dear days of love and rhyme,
Season of mirth and dance,
Love's long- lost, golden time,
Bright hair where sunshine lay
The priest's hands sheared away:
Mirror, thou know'st her well —
Hast thou, indeed, no spell
To bring her back?

But thou dost rule, O God!
Thy harvest springs from pain;
And fairest blooms are fed

On tears that fall like rain.
O Gatherer divine,
The sweetest flowers are thine!
Mirror, thou know'st her well —
Why hast thou not some spell
To bring her back?

The day she went away
Her cheeks were bathed in tears;
The long night she had wept
Past joys and future fears;
But when the convent's door
Had closed, she wept no more:
Mirror, thou know'st her well —
I seek thy magic spell
To bring her back.

Under the half-dead vine
To this porch I drew nigh:
"This House to Let," I read —
It hurt me like a cry.
No one awaits me here;
But still my heart draws near:
Mirror, thou know'st her well —
Yet thou canst work no spell
To bring her back.

LA VIE

(From the French of Montenaeken)

Ah, brief is Life,
Love's short, sweet way,
With dreamings rife,
And then — Good-day!

And Life is vain —
Hope's vague delight,
Griefs transient pain,
And then — Good-night!

www.ingramcontent.com/pod-product-compliance
Lightning Source LLC
Chambersburg PA
CBHW021941040426
42448CB00008B/1176